P9-CFN-850

D0420123

The best cosmetic in the world
is an active mind
that is always finding something new.
— Mary Meek Atkeson

Life was meant to be lived,
and curiosity must be kept alive.
One must never, for whatever reason,
turn his back on life.

— *Eleanor Roosevelt*

*I never lose an opportunity of urging
a practical beginning,
however small,
for it is wonderful how often
the mustard-seed germinates
and roots itself.*

—Florence Nightingale

Just do a thing and don't talk about it.
This is the great secret of success.

—Sarah Grand

*I believe in hard work.
It keeps the wrinkles out of the mind
and the spirit.
It helps to keep a woman young.*

— Helena Rubinstein

*As soon as you feel too old
to do a thing, do it!*

—*Margaret Deland*

The game of life
is a game of boomerangs.
Our thoughts, deeds and words
return to us sooner or later
with astounding accuracy.

—Florence Scovel Shinn

Keep your face to the sunshine
and you cannot see the shadow.
— Helen Keller

Love is like a beautiful flower whose fragrance makes the garden a place of delight.

—Helen Keller

Spend all you have for loveliness,
  Buy it and never count the cost;
For one white singing hour of peace
  Count many a year of strife well lost,
And for a breath of ecstasy
  Give all that you have been, or could be.

— Sara Teasdale
  Barter

*There is one great and universal
wish of mankind
expressed in all religions,
in all art and philosophy,
and in all human life:
the wish to pass beyond himself
as he now is.*

—Beatrice Hinkle

There are no hopeless situations;
there are only men
who have grown hopeless about them.
— Clare Boothe Luce

Every day is a fresh beginning;
  Listen, my soul, to the glad refrain,
And, in spite of old sorrow...
  and possible pain,
Take heart with the day, and begin again.
                                    — Susan Coolidge

The best way out is always through.
—Helen Keller

Every day
stop before something beautiful
long enough to say
"Isn't that b·e·a·u·t·i·f·u·l!"

—Alice Freeman Palmer

Stars over snow,
  And in the west a planet
Swinging below a star —
  Look for a lovely thing and you will find it,
It is not far —
  It never will be far.

                    — Sara Teasdale
                      Night

One ship drives east and another drives west
  With the selfsame winds that blow.
  'Tis the set of the sails
  And not the gales
Which tells us the way to go.

                                   — Ella Wheeler Wilcox

True happiness is not attained through self-gratification, but through fidelity to a worthy purpose.

—Helen Keller

Happiness is a by-product of an effort
to make someone else happy.

— Gretta Palmer

They might not need me; but they might.
I'll let my head be just in sight;
A smile as small as mine might be
Precisely their necessity.

— Emily Dickinson

*It seems to me that we can never
give up longing and wishing,
while we are thoroughly alive.
There are certain things we feel
to be beautiful and good,
and we must hunger after them.*

— George Eliot

The inner half of every cloud
  Is bright and shining;
I therefore turn my clouds about,
And always wear them inside out
  To show the lining.

— Ellen Thorneycroft Fowler

Let us be of good cheer,
remembering that the misfortunes
hardest to bear
are those which never come.

— *Amy Lowell*

"Hope" is the thing with feathers ~
That perches in the soul ~
And sings the tune without the words ~
And never stops ~ at all ~

— Emily Dickinson

Yes, I have doubted.
I have wandered off the path...
But I always return.
It is intuitive...
an intrinsic, built-in sense of
direction.
I seem always to find my way home.
My faith has wavered,
but has saved me.

—Helen Hayes

Faith is the subtle chain
which binds us to the infinite.

— *Elizabeth Oakes Smith*

When you get into a tight place
and it seems you can't go on,
hold on,
for that's just the place and the
time
that the tide will turn.

—Harriet Beecher Stowe

The force of the waves is in their perseverence.

— *Gila Guri*

God's gifts
put man's best dreams to shame.

— *Elizabeth Barrett Browning*

Keep thou thy dreams — the tissue of all wings
  Is woven first of them; from dreams are
    made
The precious and imperishable things,
  Whose loveliness lives on, and does not fade.

— Virna Sheard

The human heart yearns
for the beautiful
in all ranks of life.

—Harriet Beecher Stowe

The first condition of human goodness
is something to love;
the second, something to reverence.
— George Eliot

The soul can split the sky in two,
And let the face of God shine through.
— Edna St. Vincent Millay
from Renascence

I never saw a moor,
I never saw the sea;
Yet know I how the heather looks,
And what a wave must be.

I never spoke with God,
Nor visited in heaven;
Yet certain am I of the spot
As if the chart were given.

— Emily Dickinson

I have four things to learn in life:
to think clearly, without hurry
or confusion;
to love everybody sincerely;
to act in everything with the
highest motives;
to trust in God unhesitatingly.

— *Helen Keller*

Isn't it strange some people make
You feel so tired inside,
Your thoughts begin to shrivel up
Like leaves all brown and dried!

But when you're with some other ones,
It's stranger still to find
Your thoughts as thick as fireflies
All shiny in your mind!

—Rachel Field
Some People

God, give me sympathy and sense
And help me keep my courage high.
God, give me calm and confidence —
And, please — a twinkle in my eye.

— Margaret Bailey

The cure for all the ills and
wrongs, the cares, the sorrows and
crimes of humanity,
all lie in that one word "love."
It is the divine vitality that
produces and restores life.
To each and every one of us
it gives the power of working
miracles, if we will.

— Lydia M. Child

It is not easy to find happiness in ourselves, and impossible to find it elsewhere.

— *Agnes Repplier*

Courage is the price that life
extracts for granting peace.
The soul that knows it not knows
no release from little things.

—Amelia Earhart

Every year I live I am more convinced that the waste of life lies in the love we have not given, the powers we have not used, the selfish prudence that will risk nothing...
No one ever yet was the poorer in the long run for having once in a lifetime "let out all the length of the reins."

—Mary Cholmondeley

Talk health. The dreary, never-changing tale
Of mortal maladies is worn and stale.
You cannot charm, or interest, or please
By harping on that minor chord, disease.
Say you are well, or all is well with you,
And God shall hear your words and make
   them true.

— Ella Wheeler Wilcox

If but one message I may leave behind,
One single word of courage for my kind,
It would be this — Oh, brother, sister, friend,
Whatever life may bring — what God may send,
No matter whether clouds lift soon or late —
Take heart and wait!

— Grace Noll Crowell
Wait

Out of the earth, the rose,
  Out of the night, the dawn,
Out of my heart, with all its woes,
  High courage to press on.

— *Laura Lee Randall*

I believe in the immortality
of the soul because
I have within me immortal longings.

— *Helen Keller*

Though my soul may set in darkness,
   It will rise in perfect light,
I have loved the stars too fondly
   To be fearful of the night.

— Sarah Williams

Inspiration is a fragile thing...
who can say where it is born...
Who can tell the reasons for its
being or not being?...
I think inspiration comes from the
Heart of Heaven to give the lift of
wings, and the breath of divine
music to those of us who are earthbound.

—Margaret Sangster

Far away there in the sunshine
are my highest aspirations.
I may not reach them,
but I can look up and see their
beauty,
believe in them,
and try to follow where they lead.
—Louisa May Alcott

No vision and you perish;
  No ideal, and you're lost;
Your heart must ever cherish
  Some faith at any cost.

Some hope, some dream to cling to,
  Some rainbow in the sky,
Some melody to sing to,
  Some service that is high.

  —Harriet Du Autermont

Every day is a fresh beginning;
   Listen, my soul, to the glad refrain,
And, in spite of old sorrow...
   and possible pain,
Take heart with the day, and begin again.

— Susan Coolidge

The editor and WELLSPRING extend our thanks to the publishers listed for permission to reprint parts of works owned by them. We have taken care to trace the ownership of all the selections used, and to include the proper acknowledgment. If we have inadvertently made an error, or if an acknowledgment has been omitted, it will, of course, be corrected in future editions.

"Some People" by Rachel Field reprinted with permission of Macmillan Publishing Company from POEMS by Rachel Field. (New York: Macmillan, 1957).

"Barter" by Sara Teasdale reprinted with permission of Macmillan Publishing Company from COLLECTED POEMS OF SARA TEASDALE. Copyright 1917 by Macmillan Publishing Company, renewed 1945 by Mamie T. Wheless.

"Night" by Sara Teasdale reprinted with permission of Macmillan Publishing Company from STARS TONIGHT. Copyright 1930 by Sara Teasdale Filsinger, renewed 1958 by Guaranty Trust Co. of N.Y.

Excerpt from "Renascence" by Edna St. Vincent Millay from COLLECTED POEMS, Harper & Row Publishers, Inc. Copyright © 1912, 1944, by Edna St. Vincent Millay. Reprinted with permission.

Poems by Emily Dickinson reprinted by permission of the publishers and the Trustees of Amherst College from THE POEMS OF EMILY DICKINSON, edited by Thomas H. Johnson, Cambridge, Mass.: The Belknap Press of Harvard University Press, Copyright 1951, © 1955, 1979, 1983 by the President and Fellows of Harvard College.

Excerpt from LAST FLIGHT by Amelia Earhart, copyright 1937 by George Palmer Putnam; renewed 1965 by Mrs. George Palmer Putnam. Reprinted by permission of Harcourt Brace Jovanovich, Inc.

"Wait" copyright 1936 by Grace Noll Crowell, from POEMS OF INSPIRATION by Grace Noll Crowell. Reprinted by permission of Harper & Row Publishers, Inc.